great ideas,
gentle as doves

reflections on
Catholic social teaching

by Timothy Brown, S.J.

ISBN: 0-9668716-9-3
This book is printed on acid free paper.

First Edition, updated

Design by Erin Jones
Edited by Susan Hodges

All scripture passages have been taken from
the New Revised Standard Version of the Bible.

*Those parties involved in this publication take no responsibility
for typographical errors or misprints. Every effort was made to
ensure the accuracy of information included in this book.*

resonant publishing

Baltimore, Maryland
www.resonantgroup.com

Dedicated to...

Sister Leontine O'Gorman, R.S.C.J.
A true mentor and friend.

"Great ideas, it has been said, come into the world as gently as doves. Perhaps then, if we listen we shall hear amid the uproar of empires and nations a faith flutter of wings, a gently stirring of hope.

- *Camus*

table of contents

introduction

Wisdom 7:22-8:1

Wisdom, the fashioner of all things, taught me.
There is in her a spirit that is intelligent, holy,
unique, manifold, subtle,
mobile, clear, unpolluted,
distinct, invulnerable, loving the good,
keen, irresistible,
beneficent, humane, steadfast,
sure, free from anxiety,
all-powerful, overseeing all,
and penetrating through all spirits
that are intelligent, pure, and altogether subtle.
For wisdom is more mobile than any motion;
because of her pureness
she pervades and penetrates all things.
For she is a breath of the power of God,
and a pure emanation of the glory of the Almighty;
therefore nothing defiled gains entrance into her.
For she is a reflection of eternal light,
a spotless mirror of the working of God,
and an image of his goodness.
Although she is but one, she can do all things,
and while remaining in herself, she renews all things;
in every generation she passes into holy souls
and makes them friends of God, and prophets;
for God loves nothing so much
as the person who lives with wisdom.
She is more beautiful than the sun,
and excels every constellation of the stars.
Compared with the light she is found to be superior,
for it is succeeded by the night,
but against wisdom evil does not prevail.
She reaches mightily from one end of the earth to the other,
and she orders all things well.

Catholic Social Teaching

Just as the God of love is the God of community,
so we as a community need to try together
to understand God's teaching
about how creation should be honored.

We try to do this through the tradition
called "Catholic Social Teaching,"
frequently expressed in papal encyclicals.

In this tradition,
asking the guidance of the Holy Spirit,
and in dialogue with the community of faith,
we try to interpret God's word for today's society.

This tradition, we believe,
is a rich resource for us
as we seek to find a path of life
based on sustainable communities.

Catholic Bishops of Appalachia

Introduction

In assembling this selection of essays, prayers, and scripture passages, I hope to engage the reader in the vibrancy of Catholic Social Teaching. My thought was to collect these essays in one place and, through questions following each essay, provide the means for further reflection on these important topics.

At this point in our history, the rich tapestry of Catholic social teaching can provide a sense of direction in our lives. We all make up the fabric of life – woven together in a single cloth – and all are stewards of each other and creation as a whole.

The ideas that make up the body of Catholic Social Teaching are not new ideas. It is my hope that these selections will stimulate us to greater service to each other and to our world. That the world will begin to pay attention to this "faith flutter of wings," this "stirring of hope."

Timothy Brown, S.J.

paying attention

In Days to Come

In days to come
     the mountain of the Lord's house
Shall be established as the highest of mountains,
     and shall be raised up above the hills.
Peoples shall stream to it,
     and many nations shall come and say:
"Come, let us go up to the mountain of the LORD,
     to the house of the God of Jacob;
     that he may teach us in his ways
     and that we may walk in his paths."
For out of Zion shall go forth instruction,
     and the word of the LORD from Jerusalem.
He shall judge between many peoples
     and shall arbitrate between strong nations far away;
     they shall beat their swords into plowshares,
     and their spears into pruning hooks;
     nation shall not lift up sword against nation
     neither shall they learn war any more;
     but they shall sit under their own vines
     and under their own fig trees,
     and no one shall make them afraid;
     for the mouth of the Lord of hosts has spoken.

Micah 4:1-4

Paying Attention

I want to share with you a few thoughts regarding the role of service within the context of a Jesuit institution like Loyola College in Maryland. In the *Contemplation of the Incarnation* in the Spiritual Exercises, Saint Ignatius asks that we try to place ourselves with the Trinity, as they look down on the earth and behold persons in such great diversity in dress and manner of acting:

"Some are white, some black, some at peace, and some at war; some weeping, some laughing; some well, some sick; some coming into the world, and some dying."

I carry that image of attentiveness around with me as a way to put a perspective on service in the context of Loyola College. As a Jesuit institution, I believe our task is not only to give students the skills they need for distinguished professional performance but also to teach them to be leaders who are sensitive to justice and service and who can exercise their power with competence and compassion.

The Center for Values and Service was established to organize service outreach programs and to promote faith and education for justice through reflection and academic study. The Center strives to respond to the challenge of the leaders of our Jesuit schools issued by Peter-Hans Kolvenbach, the Superior General of the Society of Jesus, in a 1989 address. In the words of Fr. Kolvenbach: "We want graduates who will be leaders concerned about the society and the world in which they live, desirous of eliminating hunger and conflict in the world, sensitive to the need for more equitable distribution of God's bounty, seeking to end sexual and social discrimination, eager to share their faith and their love with others. In short, we want our graduates to be leaders in service." Moreover, "the service of faith through the promotion of justice...which is profoundly linked with our preferential option for the poor, [must] be operative in our lives and our institutions." To be faithful to this vision, college students – and universities themselves – must find creative ways to embrace this "preferential option for the poor" and the mandate for solidarity with people who are materially poor that it necessarily entails.

Education in service of the materially disadvantaged may,

to some, seem quite radical. But, in many ways, it follows a long-standing tradition, especially in Jesuit history, rooted in a pedagogy that distinguishes true education from simple training. We go to school not so much for knowledge alone, but rather to develop virtuous habits: the habit of expression, the habit of attention, even the habit of being. Developing these habits of virtue requires an integrated effort that involves linking service experience with rigorous classroom study. It takes practice and even concentration. Most fundamentally it requires us to cultivate the habit of paying attention.

In Waiting for God, Simone Weil develops this theme of attentiveness in an essay entitled "Reflections on the Right School Studies with a View of the Love of God." In it she explains that, for the person pursuing studies with a view to the love of God, one's sole interest and real object must be to develop the faculty of attention. She views attention as a kind of waiting, watching, and suspended thought. The point of all this is to be open to receive truth. She is interested in developing an attitude, a habit of paying attention, which I see as absolutely essential for our students, for it is this habit of contemplative attentiveness that empowers students to re-imagine the world in which we live.

Paying attention in this way requires extraordinary discipline and concentration. The capacity to give one's attention to a sufferer (to someone in need) is a very rare and difficult habit to develop – almost a miracle – and nearly all those who think they have this capacity do not possess it. To give this kind of attention means being able to say to our neighbor: "What are you going through?" To be able to pay attention to another in a community service setting challenges a student to be open to the experiences of another and to ask, "What are you about?"

Our students come to us in need of developing this habit of critically reflective attentiveness. This is essential if they are to acquire the ability to re-imagine our world in ways that reflect the Gospel values of fidelity, gratitude, compassion, self-giving love, reconciliation, hospitality, simplicity of life, inclusiveness, and respect for the dignity of each human person. At Loyola, we have a special mission, a special calling. We are challenged to make it possible for each person to seek the mark of God in all creation. We are called to make a case not only for functional literacy but for moral literacy as well: To create and foster some moral energy, moral passion, moral intelligence which says that we all can be larger than ourselves and to be able to ask the questions that are so crucial for these times.

We need to be respectfully attentive to the transcendent values of each and every person that are revealed in our encounters and relationships with others in service. It is these encounters and relationships that serve to spark the critical development of imagination. Imagination is the capacity of our hearts and minds to see meaning beyond what is immediately evident; to stretch the limits of the obvious. It is the ability to make connections, to envision possibilities. If we are to grow in our ability to imagine new possibilities for constituting good lives and good communities, it is essential that we attentively enter together into relationships and conversations in which we can encounter the lived realities and imaginative visions of others.

Developing one's moral imagination goes hand in hand with developing the ability to pay attention – to make good decisions – to find meaning in what one does. The gift of imagination allows us to see the things that we sometimes miss because of our limited attention spans. Through service with people who are materially poor, many students have begun to develop a particular vision of how the world could possibly be re-imagined. The vision – the paying attention, the "seeing as" – is very much an exercise of imagination. To reformulate their vision, many students have had to let go of pre-conceived notions of how people think, act, and live out their lives. Through their service experiences, I have seen scores of students forced to suspend past notions and impressions of the people with whom they are working; they have come to a deeper seeing of the world. I have seen students return to campus challenged by serious social problems. They have come back to Loyola stunned, sometimes confused, often times without the words to express their frustrations. With stories, metaphors, vision, and prayerful, contemplative reflection on service, imagination can offer another kind of resource – a moral resource.

Jesuit education, at its best, forms students who are able to engage in just this sort of creative re-imagining of their experiences and the world in which they live and act. And community service plays a crucial role in this education of the moral imagination. Through our service experiences, all of us – students, faculty and members of the communities in which service takes the world of others in their otherness, and in the concreteness of their diverse experience – grow in our ability to re-imagine the world we share. We "are freed to go out of ourselves and live with   others in friendship," a friendship that compels us to strive to   create communities that reverence the dignity of all people.

Timothy Brown, S.J.

Vision

Do you have a vision of God's call?
> "What does the Lord require of you but to do justice, and to love kindness, and to walk humbly with your God?"
> (Micah 6:8)

Do you have a vision of God's workers?
> "Let no one despise your youth, but set the believers an example in speech and conduct, in love, in faith, in purity."
> (1 Timothy 4:12)

Do you have a vision of God's people?

Do you have a vision of God's peace?

Do you have a vision of God's friendship?

Have you glimpsed God's vision?

Do you take seriously the words, "for it is in giving that we receive"?

Broken Cisterns

O Lord,
do not let us turn into "broken cisterns"
that can hold no water...
do not let us be so blinded by the enjoyment
        of the good things of earth
that our hearts become insensible to the cry
        of the poor,
        of the sick, or orphaned children
        and of those innumerable brothers and
                sisters of ours
        who lack the necessary minimum to eat,
        to clothe their nakedness,
        and to gather their family together under
                one roof.

Pope John XXIII

solidarity

Truly I Tell You

Then the righteous will answer him, 'Lord, when was it that we saw you hungry and gave you food, or thirsty and gave you something to drink? And when was it that we saw you a stranger and welcomed you, or naked and gave you clothing? And when was it that we saw you sick or in prison and visited you?' And the king will answer them, 'Truly I tell you, just as you did it to one of the least of these who are members of my family, you did it to me.'

Matthew 25: 37-40

The Service of Faith and the Promotion of Justice in American Jesuit Higher Education

Within the complex time and place we are in, and in the light of the recent General Congregations, I want to spell out several ideal characteristics, as manifest in three complementary dimensions of Jesuit higher education: in who our students become, in what our faculty do, and in how our universities proceed. When I speak of ideals, some are easy to meet, others remain persistently challenging, but together they serve to orient our schools and, in the long run, to identify them. At the same time, the U.S. Provincials have recently established an important Higher Education Committee to propose criteria on the staffing, leadership and Jesuit sponsorship of our colleges and universities. May these criteria help to implement the ideal characteristics we now meditate on together.

Today's predominant ideology reduces the human world to a global jungle whose primordial law is the survival of the fittest. Students who subscribe to this view want to be equipped with well-honed professional and technical skills in order to compete in the market and secure one of the relatively scarce fulfilling and lucrative jobs available. This is the success which many students (and parents!) expect.

All American universities, ours included, are under tremendous pressure to opt entirely for success in this sense. But what our students want - and deserve - includes but transcends this "worldly success" based on marketable skills. The real measure of our Jesuit universities lies in who our students become.

For four hundred and fifty years, Jesuit education has sought to educate "the whole person" intellectually and professionally, psychologically, morally and spiritually. But in the emerging global reality, with its great possibilities and deep contradictions, the whole person is different from the whole person of the Counter-Reformation, the Industrial Revolution, or the 20th Century. Tomorrow's "whole person" cannot be whole without an educated awareness of society and culture with which to contribute socially, generously, in the real world. Tomorrow's whole person must have, in brief, a well-educated solidarity.

We must therefore raise our Jesuit educational standard to "educate the whole person of solidarity for the real world." Solidarity is learned through "contact" rather than through "concepts," as the Holy Father said recently at an Italian university conference. When the heart is touched by direct experience, the mind may be challenged to change.

Students, in the course of their formation, must let the gritty reality of this world into their lives, so they can learn to feel it, think about it critically, respond to its suffering and engage it constructively. They should learn to perceive, think, judge, choose and act for the rights of others, especially the disadvantaged and the oppressed. Campus ministry does much to foment such intelligent, responsible and active compassion, compassion that deserves the name solidarity.

Our universities also boast a splendid variety of in-service programs, outreach programs, insertion programs, off-campus contacts and hands-on courses. These should not be too optional or peripheral, but at the core of every Jesuit university's program of studies.

Our students are involved in every sort of social action - tutoring drop-outs, demonstrating in Seattle, serving in soup kitchens, promoting pro-life, protesting against the School of the Americas - and we are proud of them for it. But the measure of Jesuit universities is not what our students do but who they become and the adult Christian responsibility they will exercise in future towards their neighbor and their world. For now, the activities they engage in, even with much good effect, are for their formation. This does not make the university a training camp for social activists. Rather, the students need close involvement with the poor and the marginal now, in order to learn about reality and become adults of solidarity in the future.

If the measure and purpose of our universities lies in what the students become, then the faculty are at the heart of our universities. Their mission is tirelessly to seek the truth and to form each student into a whole person of solidarity who will take responsibility for the real world. What do they need in order to fulfill this essential vocation?

The faculty's "research, which must be rationally rigorous,

firmly rooted in faith and open to dialogue with all people of good will," not only obeys the canons of each discipline, but ultimately embraces human reality in order to help make the world a more fitting place for six billion of us to inhabit. I want to affirm that university knowledge is valuable for its own sake and at the same time is knowledge that must ask itself, "For whom? For what?"

In some disciplines such as the life sciences, the social sciences, law, business, or medicine, the connections with "our time and place" may seem more obvious. These professors apply their disciplinary specialties to issues of justice and injustice in their research and teaching about health care, legal aid, public policy, and international relations. But every field or branch of knowledge has values to defend, with repercussions on the ethical level. Every discipline, beyond its necessary specialization, must engage with human society, human life, and the environment in appropriate ways, cultivating moral concern about how people ought to live together.

All professors, in spite of the cliché of the ivory tower, are in contact with the world. But no point of view is ever neutral or value-free. By preference, by option, our Jesuit point of view is that of the poor. So our professors' commitment to faith and justice entails a most significant shift in viewpoint and choice of values. Adopting the point of view of those who suffer injustice, our professors seek the truth and share their search and its results with our students. A legitimate question, even if it does not sound academic, is for each professor to ask, "When researching and teaching, where and with whom is my heart?" To expect our professors to make such an explicit option and speak about it is obviously not easy; it entails risks. But I do believe that this is what Jesuit educators have publicly stated, in Church and in society, to be our defining commitment.

To make sure that the real concerns of the poor find their place in research, faculty members need an organic collaboration with those in the Church and in society who work among and for the poor and actively seek justice. They should be involved together in all aspects: presence among the poor, designing the research, gathering the data, thinking through problems, planning and action, doing evaluation and theological reflection. In each Jesuit Province where our universities are found, the faculty's privileged working relationships should be with projects of the Jesuit social apostolate - on issues such as poverty and exclusion, housing, AIDS, ecology and Third World debt - and with the Jesuit Refugee Service helping refugees and forcibly displaced people.

Just as the students need the poor in order to learn, so the professors need partnerships with the social apostolate in order to research and teach and form. Such partnerships do not turn Jesuit universities into branch plants of social ministries or agencies of social change, as certain rhetoric of the past may have led some to fear, but are a verifiable pledge of the faculty's option and really help, as the colloquial expression goes, "to keep your feet to the fire!"

If the professors choose viewpoints incompatible with the justice of the Gospel and consider researching, teaching and learning to be separable from moral responsibility for their social repercussions, they are sending a message to their students. They are telling them that they can pursue their careers and self-interest without reference to anyone "other" than themselves.

By contrast, when faculty do take up inter-disciplinary dialogue and socially-engaged research in partnership with social ministries, they are exemplifying and modeling knowledge that is service, and the students learn by imitating them.

If the measure of our universities is who the students become, and if the faculty are the heart of it all, then what is there left to say? It is perhaps the third topic, the character of our universities - how they proceed internally and how they impact on society - which is the most difficult.

What, then, constitutes this ideal character? and what contributes to the public's perception of it? In the case of a Jesuit university, this character must surely be the mission, which is defined by GC 32 and reaffirmed by GC 34: the diakonia fidei and the promotion of justice, as the characteristic Jesuit university way of proceeding and of serving socially.

In the words of the 34th General Congregation, a Jesuit university must be faithful to both the noun "university" and to the adjective "Jesuit." To be a university requires dedication "to research, teaching and the various forms of service that correspond to its cultural mission." To be Jesuit "requires that the university act in harmony with the demands of the service of faith and promotion of justice."

The first way, historically, that our universities began living out their faith-justice commitment was through their admissions policies, affirmative action for minorities, and scholarships for disadvantaged students; and these continue to be effective means. An even more telling expression of the Jesuit university's nature is found in policies concerning hiring and tenure. As a university it is necessary to respect the established academic, professional and labor norms, but as Jesuit it is essential to go beyond them and find ways of attracting, hiring and promoting those who actively share the mission.

I believe that we have made considerable and laudable Jesuit efforts to go deeper and further: we have brought our Ignatian spirituality, our reflective capacities, some of our international resources, to bear. Good results are evident.

Very Rev. Peter-Hans Kolvenbach, S.J.
Superior General of the Society of Jesus

Reflection

What do you do to promote the faith that does justice?

How do you bring a face to the large issue of human dignity?

Are you fulfilling, post college service experiences, the essential vocation of being a person of solidarity? Who have you become?

Project Mexico

For the past decade a number of students from Loyola College in Baltimore, Maryland, have been spending their January break in Tecate and Tijuana in an enormously successful venture called Project Mexico. Twenty-five of us spent 10 days working on two construction projects: one at a Catholic boys' orphanage conducted by a remarkable group of Mexican nuns, the other in a relatively new area of Tijuana, where we helped build a kitchen-cafeteria at which children can receive one hot meal a day for about a dollar. The hope is that the cafeteria will serve as a community center for people to share goods, food, clothing and friendship.

Here is how one student described Project Mexico: "The project is a way of opening our eyes and hearts to global realities. We begin, many of us, as young people without an understanding of the full scope of human existence. In Mexico, we discovered at first hand the hard fact of extreme poverty. But the greatest discovery experienced is the compassion and kindness within the human spirit."

An instance of "opening our eyes and hearts" to "the hard fact of extreme poverty" is the following. In Mexico last year we visited a group of people in one of the colonias or "settlements." They have a tradition that on the feast of the Three Kings the children prepare a Christmas pageant, which is very important to all the people. Imagine that the poor, simple, smiling children in this obscure Mexican village shared the same sense of wonder and joy over their baby Jesus as did the shepherds and Magi 2,000 years ago.

As we know from the Gospel of Luke, no true homage to the birth of Jesus would be complete without a manger scene, and here in this village the manger scene was key to the whole Three Kings celebration. All the children played their parts, from Mary and Joseph to the shepherds. The Three Wise Men, the innkeeper and even the animals turned out to be the real thing. And a cat, some chickens and a few stray dogs also helped to form the backdrop.

As you picture this scene, you must not forget that these children were, in a real sense, very poor. The makeshift costumes worn that day were thrown-away clothes, rags pieced together. As the pageant unfolded, the children began praying and singing, and crowding closer and closer to the baby Jesus. The baby was a tiny creature a few months old, a beautiful baby boy clothed in rags. The other *niños* were practically on top of the child. I looked at the dirty ground, the animals sidling up to the infant, and then it struck me: this child – poor, dressed in rags, nearly helpless – he was the baby Jesus. This was probably truer to the actual setting and circumstances into which Jesus was born than any I had ever experienced. And that day I learned more about the reality of God's trusting love, his giving his son over to the world and to Mary.

Of my last Project Mexico experience I have several vivid, recurring recollections. One is of a small boy who dreamed of becoming an architect. Although I cannot remember his name, I am still troubled by the thought of him. I admired his sense of the future. In Mexico the peoples' daily struggles with poverty and despair leave very little time for dreams. The fact that this boy could fancy such a future was a testimonial to the *madres* who reared him. But there was no real opportunity for him to see his dream reach fruition, and this realization frustrated me. Most boys do not even attend high school because their parents cannot afford the uniforms that the schools require.

Perspectives

Such hopes can be built on gratitude. There is an ancient Aztec prayer that speaks of gratitude and the preciousness of life and its fleetingness. As the Aztecs thank their God for their life, they acknowledge that they are simply on loan to one another for a short time. They have a prayer that reads:

> Oh, only for so short a while
> You have lent us to each other,
> Because we take form in your act
> of drawing us.
> And we take life in your painting us,
> And we breathe in your singing us.
> But only for so short a while
> Have you lent us to each other.

Isn't seeing life as being on loan a great philosophy to hold? I think it helps us to be courageous, to take risks, to be adventurous and daring. When you look at life as being on loan, you look at things differently. You look at this loan for what it really is—a pure gift, pure grace given to us from God. When you look at life as a loan, material things are put into perspective.

I once heard a wise Jesuit say that it is impossible to be grateful and unhappy at the same time. When I was in Mexico last January I understood what he meant, and can remember hearing some Loyola students from that trip make similar observations. Two students of the group met Lupe and her son Federico while volunteering at La Casa de los Pobres (House of the Poor), in Tijuana. There needy people can receive two meals a day, groceries, clothing and health care. During their time at the Casa, the students became close to Lupe and Federico. On their last night in Tijuana, before joining the rest of us in Tecate, they gave Federico a small bag of toys and money. But when they took him home that evening, Federico showed them an act of generosity and self-lessness that few might expect from a seven-year-old. As soon as the little boy got into the house, he took the bag and the money and gave them to his mother to divide among the other children. That's the way everyone was. They help others before they help themselves. The philosophy of all being on loan seems to have taken place in that situation.

Another student who graduated last May had her own special story of a woman who deeply touched her. Lupita is the mother of Gustavo and Martín, two boys from the orphanage where we worked. They stayed at the orphanage because Lupita was too poor and sick to care for them. Lupita lived in one of the poorest *colonias* in Tijuana, where people attempt to survive in structures made of plastic, cardboard, tires or whatever else they can find. Part of Project Mexico's money that year went toward the construction of a new house for Lupita and her family. A woman in her 50's, Lupita has to travel down a steep hill to get water for cleaning and cooking, and despite her cancer, arthritis and high blood pressure, she must then carry the huge jugs back up the steep slope. When the small group of Loyola students went to visit Lupita for the first time, she greeted them with hugs, invited them into her house and prepared tea and coffee for them. She had little to offer but gave what little she had. That kind of hospitality made a deep impression on the students.

On January 3, another group will leave for Mexico. They are able to make the trip because of the generosity and assistance of many people at Loyola. The support for this venture has been tremendous. I think it can be said that Loyola College has demonstrated a gratitude and appreciation which mirrors that displayed by the Mexican people "What you receive as a gift—give as gift!"

After returning from their trip to Mexico over one Christmas break, students wrote down their impressions and reflections. Here are excerpts from the paper of a young man who had made the trip.

"What an amazing day! We started off going to Leander, a colonia in Tijuana, and we were to build a kindergarten building. It is so poor here, yet they have nothing but incredible love and peace with themselves. We did various activities such as construct a bathroom, put it over the septic tank and dig ditches for people."

Change the World

"You can never teach anyone something—you can only help them find it within themselves. After Mass, we spent the time talking and mixing cultures and friendship. Peace and love are given so easily by the Mexicans, and their hospitality is overwhelming...We talked to some migrants; in their reflections people spoke about being frustrated at the lack of work... Everyone was sad about what we have in comparison to them and about why they cannot get ahead. It ended on a note that it is in our hands to educate ourselves and others and to never forget what we saw. Never doubt that a small group of thoughtful, committed persons can help change the world."

"Sunday I went to an old age home run by Mother Teresa's Missionaries of Charity... We had several jobs to do here such as cleaning, feeding the handicapped, doing laundry by hand. I gave people manicures and pedicures with nail clippers. It was really not like work because there is such self-satisfaction in doing it."

"Day nine at the orphanage. We slept through the night, our next to last, listening to the windows slam and the rain pour down on Rancho Nazareth. Not even the rain, however, could hinder us totally from our tasks at hand that we wanted to finish. The roofers were desperately trying to patch all the holes, the painters groomed, and those working on the fence around the garden forgot the wind and rain to accomplish their goal. They desired to give every last effort. Time with the boys was very special before we left. It was starting to get sad, and grins were turning into faces of sorrow. Both sides of the border felt the pain that would come with our departure the next morning. But we shrugged it off until then. The next day we left. The bus drove down the hill."

"Looking back, we watched the boys run after the bus and catch their last glimpse. I can't write down all the thoughts and reactions of the last 10 days. It is too incredible. Words are not enough... God bless the people of Mexico."

Timothy Brown, S.J.

Challenges

How do you incorporate the principles of Catholic social teaching in your daily life? How do you incorporate these principles at your place of work? In your community? With your family?

How can you better promote an understanding of and respect for human dignity?

How do you work against tendencies toward "excessive individualism"? Do you build community in your corner of the world?

How aware are you of the most vulnerable members of the local community? Of your country? Do you build relationships with the poor around you?

How involved are you in local and national politics? Do you consider the needs of those living at the margins of our society when you vote?

Timothy Brown, S.J.

Sharing Catholic Social Teaching

Catholic social teaching is a central and essential element of our faith. Its roots are in the Hebrew prophets who announced God's special love for the poor and called God's people to a covenant of love and justice. Catholic social teaching is built on a commitment to the poor. This commitment arises from our experience of Christ in the Eucharist.

We believe in the triune God, whose very nature is communal and social. We who are made in God's image share this communal, social nature. We are called to reach out and to build relationships of love and justice.

Catholic social teaching is based on and inseparable from our understanding of human life and human dignity. Every human being is created in the image of God and redeemed by Jesus Christ, and therefore is invaluable and worthy of respect as a member of the human family. Human dignity comes from God, not from any human quality or accomplishment. Our commitment to the Catholic social mission must be rooted in and strengthened by our spiritual lives.

We offer these reflections to address the pressing need to educate all Catholics on the church's social teaching and to share the social demands of the Gospel and Catholic tradition more clearly. As pastors and as teachers of the faith, we ask Catholic educators and catechists to join with us in facing the urgent challenge of communicating Catholic social teaching more fully to all the members of our family of faith.

The focus of this statement is the urgent task to incorporate more fully and explicitly Catholic social teaching into Catholic educational programs. Recognizing the importance of this broader goal of Catholic education and formation, we call for a renewed commitment to integrate Catholic social teaching into the mainstream of all Catholic educational institutions and programs.

Our social doctrine is not shared or taught in a consistent and comprehensive way in too many of our schools, seminaries, religious education programs, colleges and universities. We need to build on the good work already under way to ensure that every Catholic understands how the Gospel and church teaching call us to "choose life," to serve the "least among us," to "hunger and thirst" for justice and to be "peacemakers."

Many Catholics do not adequately understand that the social teaching of the church is an essential part of Catholic faith. We need to do more to share the social mission and message of our church. Central to our identity as Catholics is that we are called to be leaven for transforming the world, agents for bringing about a kingdom of love and justice.

The church's social teaching is a rich treasure of wisdom about building a just society and living lives of holiness amid the challenges of modern society. It offers moral principles and coherent values that are badly needed in our time. We wish to highlight several of the key themes which are at the heart of our Catholic social tradition.

Life and Dignity of the Human Person

In a world warped by materialism and declining respect for human life, the Catholic Church proclaims that human life is sacred and that the dignity of the person is the foundation of a moral vision for society. Our belief in the sanctity of human life and the inherent dignity of the human person is the foundation of all the principles of our social teaching. We believe that every person is precious, that people are more important than things and that the measure of every institution is whether it threatens or enhances the life and dignity of the human person.

Call to Family, Community, Participation

In a global culture driven by excessive individualism, our tradition proclaims that the person is not only sacred but also social. How we organize our society directly affects human dignity and the capacity of individuals to grow in community. The family is the central social institution. While our society often exalts individualism, the Catholic tradition teaches that human beings grow and achieve fulfillment in community.

Rights and Responsibilities

The Catholic tradition teaches that human dignity can be protected and a healthy community can be achieved only if human rights are protected and responsibilities are met. Therefore, every person has a fundamental right to life and a right to those things required for human decency. Corresponding to these rights are duties and responsibilities – to one another, to our families and to the larger society.

Option for the Poor and Vulnerable

A basic moral test is how our most vulnerable members are faring. In a society marred by deepening divisions between rich and poor, our tradition instructs us to put the needs of the poor and vulnerable first.

Dignity of Work, Rights of Workers

The economy must serve people, not the other way around. Work is more than a way to make a living; it is a form of continuing participation in God's creation. If the dignity of work is to be protected, then the basic rights of workers must be respected – the right to productive work, to decent and fair wages, to organize and join unions, to private property and to economic initiative.

Solidarity

Our culture is tempted to turn inward, becoming indifferent and sometimes isolationist in the face of international responsibilities. Catholic social teaching proclaims that we are our brothers' and sisters' keepers, wherever they live. We are one human family. Learning to practice the virtue of solidarity means learning that "loving our neighbor" has global dimensions in an interdependent world.

Care for God's Creation

The Catholic tradition insists that we show our respect for the Creator by our stewardship of creation. Care for the earth is not just an Earth Day slogan; it is a requirement of our faith. This environmental challenge has fundamental moral and ethical dimensions which cannot be ignored.

This teaching is a complex and nuanced tradition with many other important elements. Principles like subsidiarity and the common good outline the advantages and limitations of markets, the responsibilities and limits of government, and the essential roles of voluntary associations. These principles build on the foundation of Catholic social teaching, the dignity of human life. This central Catholic principle requires that we measure every policy, every institution, every action by whether it protects human life and enhances human dignity, especially for the poor and vulnerable.

These moral values and others outlined by the church are part of a systematic moral framework and a precious intellectual heritage that we call Catholic social teaching. In a world that hungers for a sense of meaning and moral direction, this teaching offers ethical criteria for action. In a society of rapid change and often confused moral values, this teaching offers consistent moral guidance for the future.

Just as the social teaching of the church is integral to Catholic faith, the social justice dimensions of teaching are integral to Catholic education and catechesis. The commitment to human life and dignity, to human rights and solidarity is a calling every Catholic educator must share with his or her students.

The Church has the God-given mission and the unique capacity to call people to live with integrity, compassion, responsibility and concern for others. Our colleges and schools are called to share not just abstract principles, but a moral framework for everyday action. The values of the church's social teaching must not be treated as tangential or optional. They must be a core part of teaching and formation.

We strongly support new initiatives to integrate the social teachings of the church more fully into educational programs and institutions. Many do this every day. They introduce their students to issues of social justice. They encourage service to those in need and reflect on the lessons learned in that service. We support new efforts to teach our social tradition and to link service and action, charity and justice.

The report of the task force includes a series of recommendations for making the church's social teaching more intentional and explicit in all areas of Catholic education.

Sharing Catholic Social Teaching:
Challenges and Directions
U.S. Bishops' Letter (Origins, Vol 28, no 7, July 2, 1998)

Reflection

What are you doing to pass the moral test on how the most vulnerable in our society fare?

How have you chosen a life of service to the least among us?

How do you organize your daily life to have an awareness of justice issues?

Are you an "Earth Day" ecologist? Do you understand that stewardship of all creation is a faith requirement to be lived daily?

How Sweet it is to Serve

Dearest Lord, may I see you today and every day in the person of the sick, and whilst nursing them minister unto you. Though you hide yourself behind the unattractive disguise of the irritable, the exacting, the unreasonable, may I still recognize you and say: "Jesus, my patient, how sweet it is to serve you."

Sweetest Lord, make me appreciative of the dignity of my high vocation, and its many responsibilities. Never permit me to disgrace it by giving way to coldness, unkindness, or impatience.

And while you are Jesus, my patient, deign also to be to me a patient Jesus, bearing with my faults, looking only to my intention, which is to love and serve you in the person of each of your sick.

Lord, increase my faith, bless my efforts and work, now and for evermore.

Mother Teresa of Calcutta

meditation on
human rights

Fast that Pleases

Is not this the fast that I choose:
        to loose the bonds of injustice,
        to undo the thongs of the yoke,
   to let the oppressed go free,
   and to break every yoke?
Is it not to share your bread
        with the hungry,
   and bring the homeless poor into
        your house;
   when you see the naked, to cover them,
   and not to hide yourself from
        your own kin?
If you offer your food to the hungry
   and satisfy the needs of the afflicted,
   then your light shall rise in the darkness
   and your gloom be like the noonday.

Isaiah 58:6-7, 10

Universal Declaration of Human Rights

Preamble

Whereas recognition of the inherent dignity and of the equal and inalienable rights of all members of the human family is the foundation of freedom, justice and peace in the world,

Whereas disregard and contempt for human rights have resulted in barbarous acts which have outraged the conscience of mankind, and the advent of a world in which human beings shall enjoy freedom of speech and belief and freedom from fear and want has been proclaimed as the highest aspiration of the common people,

Whereas it is essential, if man is not to be compelled to have recourse, as a last resort, to rebellion against tyranny and oppression, that human rights should be protected by the rule of law,

Whereas it is essential to promote the development of friendly relations between nations,

Whereas the peoples of the United Nations have in the Charter reaffirmed their faith in fundamental human rights, in the dignity and worth of the human person and in the equal rights of men and women and have determined to promote social progress and better standards of life in larger freedom,

Whereas Member States have pledged themselves to achieve, in co-operation with the United Nations, the promotion of universal respect for and observance of human rights and fundamental freedoms,

Whereas a common understanding of these rights and freedoms is of the greatest importance for the full realization of this pledge,

Now, Therefore THE GENERAL ASSEMBLY proclaims THIS UNIVERSAL DECLARATION OF HUMAN RIGHTS as a common standard of achievement for all peoples and all nations, to the end that every individual and every organ of society, keeping this Declaration constantly in mind, shall strive by teaching and education to promote respect for these rights and freedoms and by progressive measures, national and international, to secure their universal and effective recognition and observance, both among the peoples of Member States themselves and among the peoples of territories under their jurisdiction.

Article 1.

All human beings are born free and equal in dignity and rights. They are endowed with reason and conscience and should act towards one another in a spirit of brotherhood.

Article 2.

Everyone is entitled to all the rights and freedoms set forth in this Declaration, without distinction of any kind, such as race, colour, sex, language, religion, political or other opinion, national or social origin, property, birth or other status. Furthermore, no distinction shall be made on the basis of the political, jurisdictional or international status of the country or territory to which a person belongs, whether it be independent, trust, non-self-governing or under any other limitation of sovereignty.

Article 3.

Everyone has the right to life, liberty and security of person.

Article 4.

No one shall be held in slavery or servitude; slavery and the slave trade shall be prohibited in all their forms.

Article 5.

No one shall be subjected to torture or to cruel, inhuman or degrading treatment or punishment.

Article 6.

Everyone has the right to recognition everywhere as a person before the law.

Article 7.

All are equal before the law and are entitled without any discrimination to equal protection of the law. All are entitled to equal protection against any discrimination in violation of this Declaration and against any incitement to such discrimination.

Article 8.

Everyone has the right to an effective remedy by the competent national tribunals for acts violating the fundamental rights granted him by the constitution or by law.

Article 9.

No one shall be subjected to arbitrary arrest, detention or exile.

Article 10.

Everyone is entitled in full equality to a fair and public hearing by an independent and impartial tribunal, in the determination of his rights and obligations and of any criminal charge against him.

Article 11.

(1) Everyone charged with a penal offence has the right to be presumed innocent until proved guilty according to law in a public trial at which he has had all the guarantees necessary for his defence.

(2) No one shall be held guilty of any penal offence on account of any act or omission which did not constitute a penal offence, under national or international law, at the time when it was committed. Nor shall a heavier penalty be imposed than the one that was applicable at the time the penal offence was committed.

Article 12.

No one shall be subjected to arbitrary interference with his privacy, family, home or correspondence, nor to attacks upon his honour and reputation. Everyone has the right to the protection of the law against such interference or attacks.

Article 13.

(1) Everyone has the right to freedom of movement and residence within the borders of each state.

(2) Everyone has the right to leave any country, including his own, and to return to his country.

Article 14.
   (1) Everyone has the right to seek and to enjoy in other countries asylum from persecution.
   (2) This right may not be invoked in the case of prosecutions genuinely arising from non-political crimes or from acts contrary to the purposes and principles of the United Nations.

Article 15.
   (1) Everyone has the right to a nationality.
   (2) No one shall be arbitrarily deprived of his nationality nor denied the right to change his nationality.

Article 16.
   (1) Men and women of full age, without any limitation due to race, nationality or religion, have the right to marry and to found a family. They are entitled to equal rights as to marriage, during marriage and at its dissolution.
   (2) Marriage shall be entered into only with the free and full consent of the intending spouses.
   (3) The family is the natural and fundamental group unit of society and is entitled to protection by society and the State.

Article 17.
   (1) Everyone has the right to own property alone as well as in association with others.
   (2) No one shall be arbitrarily deprived of his property.

Article 18.
   Everyone has the right to freedom of thought, conscience and religion; this right includes freedom to change his religion or belief, and freedom, either alone or in community with others and in public or private, to manifest his religion or belief in teaching, practice, worship and observance.

Article 19.
   Everyone has the right to freedom of opinion and expression; this right includes freedom to hold opinions without interference and to seek, receive and impart information and ideas through any media and regardless of frontiers.

Article 20.

(1) Everyone has the right to freedom of peaceful assembly and association.

(2) No one may be compelled to belong to an association.

Article 21.

(1) Everyone has the right to take part in the government of his country, directly or through freely chosen representatives.

(2) Everyone has the right of equal access to public service in his country.

(3) The will of the people shall be the basis of the authority of government; this will shall be expressed in periodic and genuine elections which shall be by universal and equal suffrage and shall be held by secret vote or by equivalent free voting procedures.

Article 22.

Everyone, as a member of society, has the right to social security and is entitled to realization, through national effort and international co-operation and in accordance with the organization and resources of each State, of the economic, social and cultural rights indispensable for his dignity and the free development of his personality.

Article 23.

(1) Everyone has the right to work, to free choice of employment, to just and favourable conditions of work and to protection against unemployment.

(2) Everyone, without any discrimination, has the right to equal pay for equal work.

(3) Everyone who works has the right to just and favourable remuneration ensuring for himself and his family an existence worthy of human dignity, and supplemented, if necessary, by other means of social protection.

(4) Everyone has the right to form and to join trade unions for the protection of his interests.

Article 24.

Everyone has the right to rest and leisure, including reasonable limitation of working hours and periodic holidays with pay.

Article 25.

(1) Everyone has the right to a standard of living adequate for the health and well-being of himself and of his family, including food, clothing, housing and medical care and necessary social services, and the right to security in the event of unemployment, sickness, disability, widowhood, old age or other lack of livelihood in circumstances beyond his control.

(2) Motherhood and childhood are entitled to special care and assistance. All children, whether born in or out of wedlock, shall enjoy the same social protection.

Article 26.

(1) Everyone has the right to education. Education shall be free, at least in the elementary and fundamental stages. Elementary education shall be compulsory. Technical and professional education shall be made generally available and higher education shall be equally accessible to all on the basis of merit.

(2) Education shall be directed to the full development of the human personality and to the strengthening of respect for human rights and fundamental freedoms. It shall promote understanding, tolerance and friendship among all nations, racial or religious groups, and shall further the activities of the United Nations for the maintenance of peace.

(3) Parents have a prior right to choose the kind of education that shall be given to their children.

Article 27.

(1) Everyone has the right freely to participate in the cultural life of the community, to enjoy the arts and to share in scientific advancement and its benefits.

(2) Everyone has the right to the protection of the moral and material interests resulting from any scientific, literary or artistic production of which he is the author.

Article 28.

Everyone is entitled to a social and international order in which the rights and freedoms set forth in this Declaration can be fully realized.

Article 29.

(1) Everyone has duties to the community in which alone the free and full development of his personality is possible.

(2) In the exercise of his rights and freedoms, everyone shall be subject only to such limitations as are determined by law solely for the purpose of securing due recognition and respect for the rights and freedoms of others and of meeting the just requirements of morality, public order and the general welfare in a democratic society.

(3) These rights and freedoms may in no case be exercised contrary to the purposes and principles of the United Nations.

Article 30.

Nothing in this Declaration may be interpreted as implying for any State, group or person any right to engage in any activity or to perform any act aimed at the destruction of any of the rights and freedoms set forth herein.

Adopted and proclaimed by the
United Nations' General Assembly
resolution 217 A (III) of 10 December 1948

Reflection

What can each of us do to make this document a living reality in our world?

How does this declaration call you to assume a role in protecting the dignity of human life?

What in this document inspires you to action?

Meditation on Human Rights

December 10, 1998, marked the 50th anniversary of the United Nations' proclamation of the Universal Declaration of Human Rights. Pope John Paul II noted that this Declaration is one of the highest expressions of the human conscience of our time. The Church has always championed human rights in light of her concern for the dignity of every human person. We have a special mission, a special calling: we are called to help each of us to seek the mark of God in all creation and to create and foster moral energy, moral passion, and moral intelligence. This concern for moral issues and values is at its heart a habit of reflection – the cultivation of practical wisdom – rather than a discrete examination of topics or issues.

I believe that the intellectual encounter can be understood according to the following useful model: a progression from experience through understanding to judgment and finally to action. The service-learning experience should provoke a need for understanding. Too often undergraduates engaged in community service feel their experiences very deeply, but think of them somewhat less deeply. In the words of T.S. Eliot, "We had the experience, but miss the meaning." Within this context, I would like to offer an opportunity for you to meditate on the U.N. Declaration of Human Rights and the words of three recent Nobel Laureates in Literature – Najib Mahfuz, Toni Morrison, and Wislawa Szymborska.

Timothy Brown, S.J.

Cleansing Humanity of Moral Pollution

From the United Nations Universal Declaration of Human Rights
Article 1. All human beings are born free and equal in dignity and rights. They are endowed with reason and conscience and should act towards one another in a spirit of brotherhood.

Nobel Lecture 1988 - Najib Mahfuz
The human mind now assumes the task of eliminating all causes of destruction and annihilation. And just as scientists exert themselves to cleanse the environment of industrial pollution, intellectuals ought to exert themselves to cleanse humanity of moral pollution...Today the greatness of a civilized leader ought to be measured by the universality of his vision and his sense of responsibility towards all human kind. The developed world and the third world are but one family. Each human being bears responsibility towards it by the degree of what he has obtained of knowledge, wisdom, and civilization. I would not be exceeding the limits of my duty if I told [the leaders of the civilized world] in the name of the third world: Be not spectators to our miseries. You have to play therein a noble role befitting your status. From your position of superiority you are responsible for any misdirection of animal, or plant, to say nothing of Man, in any of the four corners of the world. We have had enough of words. Now is the time for action. It is time to end the age of brigands and usurers. We are in the age of leaders responsible for the whole globe.

On-Line Source:
http://www.nobel.se/literature/laureates/1988/mahfouz-lecture.html

1. Are you simply going to be a spectator to human misery?

2. To what role are you called in helping to alleviate human suffering?

3. How is your education preparing you to be an advocate for human rights?

Language for Peace versus Language of Violence

From the United Nations Universal Declaration of Human Rights
Article 19. Everyone has the right to freedom of opinion and expression; this right includes freedom to hold opinions without interference and to seek, receive and impart information and ideas through any media and regardless of frontiers.

Nobel Lecture 1993 – Toni Morrison
[In her Nobel address, Toni Morrison refers to a wise old storyteller.]

She is convinced that when language dies, out of carelessness, disuse, indifference, and absence of esteem, or killed by fiat, not only she herself but all users and makers are accountable for its demise. In her country children have bitten their tongues off and use bullets instead to iterate the void of speechlessness, of disabled and disabling language, of language adults have abandoned altogether as a device for grappling with meaning, providing guidance, or expressing love. But she knows tongue-suicide is not only the choice of children. It is common among the infantile heads of state and power merchants whose evacuated language leaves them with no access to what is left of their human instincts, for they speak only to those who obey, or in order to force obedience.

The systematic looting of language can be recognized by the tendency of its users to forgo its nuanced, complex, mid-wifery properties, replacing them with menace and subjugation. Oppressive language does more than represent violence; it is violence; does more than represent the limits of knowledge; it limits knowledge. Whether it is obscuring state language or the faux language of mindless media; whether it is the proud but calcified language of the academy or the commodity-driven language of science; whether it is the malign language of law-without-ethics, or language designed for the estrangement of minorities, hiding its racist plunder in its literary cheek – it must be rejected, altered and exposed. It is the language that drinks blood, laps vulnerabilities, tucks its fascist boots under crinolines of respectability and patriotism as it moves relentlessly toward the bottom line and the bottomed-out mind.

On-Line Source:
http://www.nobel.se/literature/laureates/1993/morrison-lecture.html

1. Take a moment to examine the choice of words you use when conflict arises. Do your words reflect respect for human dignity or not?

2. What are some words that you use that can heighten greater respect in our culture?

3. How do you challenge others who use words and jokes to demean groups of people who are different from yourself?

Inspiration and Vision

From the United Nations Universal Declaration of Human Rights

Article 2. Everyone is entitled to all the rights and freedoms set forth in this Declaration, without distinction of any kind, such as race, color, sex, language, religion, political or other opinion, national or social origin, property, birth or other status. Furthermore, no distinction shall be made on the basis of the political, jurisdictional or international status of the country or territory to which a person belongs, whether it be independent, trust, non-self-governing or under any other limitation of sovereignty.

Article 3. Everyone has the right to life, liberty and security of person.

Article 25. (1) Everyone has the right to a standard of living adequate for the health and well-being of himself and of his family, including food, clothing, housing and medical care and necessary social services, and the right to security in the event of unemployment, sickness, disability, widowhood, old age or other lack of livelihood in circumstances beyond his control.

Nobel Lecture 1996 - Wislawa Szymborska

When I'm asked about this [inspiration] on occasion, I hedge the question too. But my answer is this: inspiration is not the exclusive privilege of poets or artists generally. There is, has been, and will always be a certain group of people whom inspiration visits. It's made up of all those who've consciously chosen their calling and do their job with love and imagination. It may include doctors, teachers, gardeners – and I could list a hundred more professions. Their work becomes one continuous adventure as long as they manage to keep discovering new challenges in it. Difficulties and setbacks never quell their curiosity. A swarm of new questions emerges from every problem they solve. Whatever inspiration is, it's born from a continuous "I don't know."

At this point, though, certain doubts may arise in my audience. All sorts of torturers, dictators, fanatics, and demagogues struggling for power by way of a few loudly shouted slogans also enjoy their jobs, and they too perform their duties with inventive fervor. Well, yes, but they "know." They know, and whatever they know is enough for them once and for all. They don't want to find out about anything else, since that might diminish their arguments' force. And any knowledge that doesn't lead to new questions quickly dies out: it fails to maintain the temperature required for sustaining life. In the most extreme cases, cases well known from ancient and modern history, it even poses a lethal threat to society.

I sometimes dream of situations that can't possibly come true. I audaciously imagine, for example, that I get a chance to chat with the Ecclesiastes, the author of that moving lament on the vanity of all human endeavors. I would bow very deeply before him, because he is, after all, one of the greatest poets, for me at least. That done, I would grab his hand. "'There's nothing new under the sun': that's what you wrote, Ecclesiastes. But you yourself were born new under the sun. And the poem you created is also new under the sun, since no one wrote it down before you. And all your readers are also new under the sun, since those who lived before you couldn't read your poem...And Ecclesiastes, I'd also like to ask you what new thing under the sun you're planning to work on now? A further supplement to the thoughts you've already expressed? Or maybe you're tempted to contradict some of them now? In your earlier work you mentioned joy – so what if it's fleeting? So maybe your new-under-the-sun poem will be about joy? Have you taken notes yet, do you have drafts? I doubt you'll say, 'I've written everything down, I've got nothing left to add.' There's no poet in the world who can say this, least of all a great poet like yourself."

On-Line Source:
http://www.nobel.se/literature/laureates/1996/szymborska-lecture.html

1. Who has inspired you to take up a profession that can improve the lives of those who are suffering in the world?

2. What inspires you to go beyond the question of "I don't know"?

3. How has scripture challenged you to be creative in fulfilling your duties as a steward of God's creation?

Justice in the World

Justice in the World
Synod of Bishops, Second General Assembly
November 30, 1971

We have questioned ourselves about the mission of the
People of God to further justice in the world. Even though it is
not for us to elaborate a very profound analysis of the situation of
the world, we have nevertheless been able to perceive the serious
injustices which are building around the world of men a network
of domination, oppression and abuses which stifle freedom and
which keep the greater part of humanity from sharing in the building up and enjoyment of a more just and more fraternal world.
At the same time we have noted the inmost stirring moving the
world in its depths. Movements among people are seen which
express hope in a better world and a will to change whatever has
become intolerable.

Action on behalf of justice and participation in the transformation of the world fully appear to us as a constitutive dimension of
the preaching of the Gospel, or, in other words, of the Church's
mission for the redemption of the human race and its liberation
from every oppressive situation.

Crisis of Universal Solidarity

The world in which the Church lives and acts is held captive
by a tremendous paradox. Never before have the forces working
for bringing about a unified world society appeared so powerful
and dynamic; they are rooted in the awareness of the full basic
equality as well as of the human dignity of all. People are beginning to grasp a new and more radical dimension of unity; for they
perceive that their resources are not infinite, but on the contrary
must be saved and preserved as a unique patrimony belonging to
all mankind.

The paradox lies in the fact that within this perspective of
unity the forces of division and antagonism seem today to be
increasing in strength. Ancient divisions between nations and
empires, between races and classes, today possess new technolog-

ical instruments of destruction. Unless combated and overcome by social and political action, the influence of the new industrial and technological order favors the concentration of wealth, power and decision-making in the hands of a small public or private controlling group. Economic injustice and lack of social participation keep a man from attaining his basic human and civil rights. The strong drive towards global unity, the unequal distribution which places decisions concerning three quarters of income, investment and trade in the hands of one third of the human race, namely the more highly developed part, the insufficiency of a merely economic progress, and the new recognition of the material limits of the biosphere – all this makes us aware of the fact that in today's world new modes of understanding human dignity are arising.

The Right to Development

In the face of international systems of domination, the bringing about of justice depends more and more on the determined will for development. In the developing nations and in the so-called socialist world, that determined will asserts itself especially in a struggle for forms of claiming one's rights and self-expression, a struggle caused by the evolution of the economic system itself.

This aspiring to justice asserts itself in advancing beyond the threshold at which begins a consciousness of enhancement of personal worth. This is expressed in an awareness of the right to development. It demands that the general condition of being marginal in society be overcome, so that an end will be put to the systematic barriers and vicious circles which oppose the collective advance towards enjoyment of adequate remuneration of the factors of production, and which strengthen the situation of discrimination with regard to access to opportunities and collective services from which a great part of the people are now excluded. That right to development is above all a right to hope according to the concrete measure of contemporary humanity.

By taking their future into their own hands through a determined will for progress, the developing peoples will authentically manifest their own personalization. It is impossible to conceive true progress without recognizing the necessity – within the political system chosen – of a development composed both of economic growth and participation; and the necessity too of an increase in wealth implying as well social progress by the entire community as it overcomes regional imbalance and islands of prosperity. If modernization is accepted with the intention that it serve the good of the nation, people will be able to create a culture which will constitute a true heritage of their own in the manner of a true social memory, one which is active and formative of authentic creative personality in the assembly of nations.

Voiceless Injustices

Our action is to be directed above all at those people and nations which because of various forms of oppression and because of the present character of our society are silent, indeed voiceless, victims of injustice. Take, for example, the case of migrants. To be especially lamented also is the condition of so many millions of refugees, and of every group of people suffering persecution – sometimes in institutionalized form – for racial or ethnic origin or on tribal grounds.

In many areas justice is seriously injured with regard to people who are suffering persecution for their faith, or who are in many ways being ceaselessly subjected by political parties and public authorities to an action of oppressive atheization, or who are deprived of religious liberty. Justice is also being violated by forms of oppression, both old and new, springing from restriction of the rights of individuals. The fight against legalized abortion and against the imposition of contraceptives and the pressures exerted against war are significant forms of defending the right to life. Nor should we forget the growing number of persons who are often abandoned by their families and by the community.

The Need for Dialogue

To obtain true unity of purpose, a mediatory role is essential to overcome day by day the opposition, obstacles and ingrained privileges which are to be met with in the advance towards a more human society. But effective mediation involves the creation of a lasting atmosphere of dialogue.

The Gospel Message and the Mission of the Church

In the face of the present-day situation of the world, marked as it is by the grave sin of injustice, we recognize both our responsibility and our inability to overcome it by our own strength.

The Saving Justice of God Through Christ

In the Old Testament God reveals himself to us as the liberator of the oppressed and the defender of the poor, demanding from people faith in him and justice towards one's neighbor. By his action and teaching Christ united in an indivisible way the relationship of persons to God and the relationship of people to other people. Christ lived his life in the world as a total giving of himself to God for the salvation and liberation of people. From the beginning the Church has lived and understood the Death and Resurrection of Christ as a call by God to conversion in the faith of Christ and in fraternal love, perfected in mutual help even to the point of a voluntary sharing of material goods.

According to St. Paul, the whole of the Christian life is summed up in faith affecting that love and service of neighbor which involve the fulfillment of the demands of justice. The Christian lives under the interior law of liberty, which is a permanent call to man to turn away from self-sufficiency to confidence in God and from concern for self to a sincere love of neighbor. Thus takes place genuine liberation and the gift of freedom of others. Christian love of neighbor and justice cannot be separated. For love implies an absolute demand for justice, namely a recognition of the dignity and rights of one's neighbor. Justice attains its inner fullness only in love. Unless the Christian message of love and justice shows its effectiveness through action in the cause of justice in the world, it will only with difficulty gain credibility with the people of our times.

The Mission of the Church, Hierarchy and Christians

The Church has the right, indeed the duty, to proclaim justice on the social, national and international level, and to denounce instances of injustice, when the fundamental rights of people and their very salvation demand it. Her mission involves defending and promoting the dignity and fundamental rights of the human person. The members of the Church, as members of society, have the same right and duty to promote the common good as do other citizens.

The Church's Witness

Many Christians are drawn to give authentic witness on behalf of justice by various modes of action for justice, action inspired by love in accordance with the grace which they have received from God. The Church recognizes everyone's right to suitable freedom of expression and thought. This includes the right of everyone to be heard in a spirit of dialogue which preserves a legitimate diversity within the Church.

In regard to temporal possessions, whatever be their use, it must never happen that the evangelical witness which the Church is required to give becomes ambiguous. Our faith demands of us a certain sparingness in use, and the Church is obliged to live and administer its own goods in such a way that the Gospel is proclaimed to the poor. If instead the Church appears to be among the rich and the powerful of this world its credibility is diminished.

Educating to Justice

Educational method must be such as to teach people to live their lives in its entire reality and in accord with the evangelical principles of personal and social morality which are expressed in the vital Christian witness of one's life. The method of education very frequently still in use today encourages narrow individualism. Part of the human family lives immersed in a mentality which exalts possessions. Education demands a renewal of heart. It will inculcate a truly and entirely human way of life in justice, love and simplicity. It will likewise awaken a critical sense, which will lead us to reflect on the society in which we live and on its values.

Since this education makes people decidedly more human, it will help them to be no longer the object of manipulation by communications media or political forces. It will instead enable them to take in hand their own destinies and bring about communities which are truly human. Accordingly, this education is deservedly called a continuing education, for it concerns every person and every age. It is also a practical education: it comes through action, participation and vital contact with the reality of injustice.

Education for justice is imparted first in the family. The content of this education necessarily involves respect for the person

and for his dignity. The basic principles whereby the influence of
the Gospel has made itself felt in contemporary social life are to
be found in the body of teaching set out in a gradual and timely
way from the encyclical *Rerum Novarum* to the letter *Octogesima
Adveniens*. The Church has, through *Gaudium et Spes*, better understood the situation in the modern world, in which the
Christian works out his salvation by deeds of justice. *Pacem in
Terris* gave us an authentic charter of human rights. In *Mater et
Magistra* international justice begins to take first place; it finds
more elaborate expression in *Populorum Progressio*, in the form
of a true and suitable treatise on the right to development, and
in *Octogesima Adveniens* is found a summary of guidelines for
political action.

Cooperation Between Local Churches

That the Church may really be the sign of that solidarity
which the family of nations desires, it should show in its own
life greater cooperation between the Churches of rich and poor
regions through spiritual communion and division of human and
material resources. This planning must in no way be restricted to
economic programs; it should instead stimulate activities capable
of developing that human and spiritual formation which will serve
as the leaven needed for the integral development of the human
being.

Ecumenical Collaboration

We very highly commend cooperation with our separated
Christian sisters and brothers for the promotion of justice in the
world, for bringing about development of peoples and for estab-
lishing peace. This cooperation concerns first and foremost activities for securing human dignity and fundamental rights, especially
the right to religious liberty. In the same spirit we likewise commend collaboration with all believers in God in the fostering of
social justice, peace and freedom; indeed we commend collaboration also with those who, even though they do not recognize
the Author of the world, nevertheless, in their esteem for human
values, seek justice sincerely and by honorable means.

Reflection

What can you do to give voice to the voiceless?

What do you do to overcome all the obstacles – real or imagined – and the ingrained privileges to take action?

What do you do to get out of your comfort zone and work for justice?

Make Us Worthy

Make us worthy, Lord, to serve
our fellow men and women
throughout the world
who live and die in poverty and hunger.
Give them through our hands,
this day their daily bread,
and by our understanding love,
give peace and joy. Amen.

Prayer of Pope Paul VI

to hunger and
 thirst for justice

Blessed Are They

When Jesus saw the crowds, he went up the mountain; and after he sat down, his disciples came to him. Then he began to speak, and taught them, saying: "Blessed are the poor in spirit, for theirs is the kingdom of heaven. Blessed are those who mourn, for they will be comforted. Blessed are the meek, for they will inherit the earth. Blessed are those who hunger and thirst for righteousness, for they will be filled. Blessed are the merciful, for they will receive mercy. Blessed are the pure in heart, for they will see God. Blessed are the peacemakers, for they will be called children of God. Blessed are those who are persecuted for righteousness' sake, for theirs is the kingdom of heaven. Blessed are you when people revile you and persecute you and utter all kinds of evil against you falsely on my account. Rejoice and be glad, for your reward is great in heaven, for in the same way they persecuted the prophets who were before you. You are the salt of the earth; but if salt has lost its taste, how can its saltiness be restored? It is no longer good for anything, but is thrown out and trampled under foot. You are the light of the world. A city built on a hill cannot be hid. No one after lighting a lamp puts it under the bushel basket, but on the lampstand, and it gives light to all in the house."

Matthew 5:1-15

To Hunger and Thirst for Justice

I. Justice Defined

I would like to provide you with the Ignatian approach to reflection, contemplation and meditation.

My first meditation is from a passage from Micah:

> *He has told you, O mortal, what is good;*
> *and what does the Lord require of you but*
> *to do justice, and to love kindness, and to*
> *walk humbly with your God?*
> *– Micah 6:8*

It is a courtroom scene in which there are three main figures. The prophet Micah, God, and the people of Judah. The scene opens with the figure of God acting as a pleader in court. God is calling to the mountains, the hills, and the very foundation of the earth to testify against the people. Then God goes on to indict the Kingdom of Judea, not by going through detailed offenses but going back in history, in memory about all the ways in which this relationship had gone so well and has now soured. God takes us back to the time in the desert, to the time of Exodus, to those times of saving justice and mercy, and now the people have turned a different way. Then Micah gets up, and in his own way, attempts to defend the people. God will not hear it. Finally there is a resolution as they begin to see the big picture, and those lines that we prayed this morning reversed the people once again.

This is all God requires of you. Act justly. Love tenderly. Walk humbly. Humility, tenderness, and justice. The definition, because we always need a definition to give us a focus, is a Biblical definition of justice. Justice to the demands of a relationship. What I think is important is that it is played through your own spirit and soul, and maybe goes further out.

It was `a people,' and we could talk about it in terms of our campuses. It wasn't about one on one. It was about hospitality demanded of all to those members of society. The question becomes how do we actually encourage right relationships in a society that seems to support individuality? Isn't that why so many of us were drawn to higher education? So as to be able to work together for something bigger. Think about the notion of justice in terms of fairness. What is fair and unfair? Justice, as it is understood in the biblical tradition, is best described as fidelity to the demands of a relationship. The justice of God's reign calls us to respond to God's faithful love to us through our own faithfulness to a rich network of relationships: we are to establish and maintain right relationships with God, with our sisters and brothers, and with the whole of created reality. This fidelity demands that we engage in the work of reconciliation by seeking to overturn those social realities - division, alienation, dissension, oppression, and marginalization - that cause rupture and disintegration in this community of relationships. A faith that looks to the embodied reality of God's reign generates communities that counter social conflict and disintegration. From faith comes the justice willed by God, the entry of the human family into peace and with one another.

T.S. Eliot has a great line; "We had the experience but miss the meaning." I think at this point, at least in our work with service learning and community service at Loyola in Baltimore, we got to that point. We actually need to stop the frenetic activity, literally, and do a little examen and figure out what it is we are doing. It's not as if we haven't done some of that, but we need to in a deeper way. I'll give you a little definition about contemplation. Contemplation is the long, loving look at the real. You look at that in light of acting, walking and loving.

The student with the prepared mind then knows how to discern, knows how to separate that which is essential from the non-essential. That is what this talk is, weeding out, sorting out what is essential.

I read recently a reflection on the meaning of justice from Igino Girodan, a member of the Italian parliament. He used the Beatitudes and after that Beatitude, "Blessed are those who hunger and thirst for justice for they shall have their fill," he said, "Justice is to the Christian what food is to the hungry, and drink to the thirsty." Apply your senses to that, especially your sense of taste. Justice is to the Christian as what food is to the hungry and drink to the thirsty. One who is hungry eats to the last crumb. One who is thirsty drinks to the last drop. The desire for justice must be no less than starving for it. Just as every day there is a need of food, so every day there's need of justice.

The Beatitude implies that unhappiness resides not so much in the lack of justice as in the scant appetite women and men feel for it. That sort of goes back to the old days when they made us feel still guilty about a lot of things. And I told the students, I don't want to make you feel guilty about what we have, but I want you to think about that and be careful when you talk about justice and when you think it and what it means. What does it mean to be hungry? To hunger, desire, strive, and have you really had the need to do that. And how can I help, how can we walk into a community where that is the stark reality, even for a week, is that really a good thing to do. To walk humbly.

There is a point in which that meditation, that appetite for justice, that hunger, that starving may not be something personal; I'll give an example. Fortunately we're using a book and I think it is a great book for the first year students coming in a few weeks. The book is called *Amazing Grace* by Jonathan Kozol.

Amazing Grace is a book about the hearts of children who grow up in the South Bronx - the poorest congressional district of our nation. The children we meet through the deepening friendships that evolve between Jonathan Kozol and their families defy the stereotypes of urban youth too frequently presented on TV and in newspapers.

"How old would you like to live to be?"
The 13-year-old named Anthony says, "That's easy, 113."
"That number is quite exact. How did you decide on that?"
"Well, I'm 13 and I'd like to live another 100 years."
"Why exactly 100 years?"
"I would like to live to see the human race grow-up."
The boy gets up abruptly from the bench, starts to pace around, and peers into the garden and says, "Mr. Jonathan, I committed sins."

And still standing behind this tree, behind Kozol.

Kozol says *"Big sins?"*

"Big enough."

"How big?"

"Well, not murder, but I did some things I'm not supposed to do." *"Anthony, what sins did you commit?"*

"I've taken food I wasn't supposed to have," he says.

"Are you hungry sometimes?"

 "Yes."

"What do you eat for dinner?"

"Oatmeal."

"Hot oatmeal?"

"No cold."

"With milk?"

"No, plain."

"Do you like it?"

"S'Not bad."

"What do you do if you are so hungry?"

"I go to my grandmothers or I come here to church where we get food."

"Have you ever stolen food?"

"Yes."

"Did anyone see you?"

"You think no one sees but someone sees."

"You feel guilty when you do this?"

"Yes."

"What do you do?"

"I pray to God to forgive me."

"Do you think that God is angry when you do this?"

And he comes out from behind the tree and he answers Kozol like this, *"If someone commits a sin, God turns his back on you because God is disappointed, feels sad. But if you ask God for forgiveness, it's as if you're knocking on God's door, hello wake up it's me. Are you still mad? Then God may turn to you again and give you forgiveness."*

"Do you forgive people who hurt you?"

"I try, but I'm not as strong as God. If I had the power, I would give everyone a second chance."

Timothy Brown, S.J.

Sources:
Girodan, Igino.
The Social Message of Jesus

Kozol, Jonathan
Amazing Grace
Crown Publishers, Inc.
New York. 1995

Morrison, Toni
The Dancing Mind
Alfred Knopf
New York. 1997

Strong Truths Well Lived
New Student Planner 2000-2001
"The Examen"
Pg. 13. 2001

Christ Question

Is not life more than food, and the body more than clothing? (Matthew 7:25)

Look at the birds of the air; they neither sow nor reap nor gather into barns, and yet your heavenly father feeds them. Are you not of more value than they? (Matthew 7:26)

Can any of you by worrying add a single hour to your span of life? (Matthew 7:27)

And why do you worry about clothing? (Matthew 7:28)

If God so clothes the grass of the field, which is alive today and tomorrow is thrown into the oven, will he not much more clothe you – you of little faith? (Matthew 7:30)

Why do you see the speck in your neighbor's eye, but do not notice the log in your own eye? (Matthew 7:3)

And he said to them, "Why are you afraid, you of little faith?" (Matthew 8:26)

And he said to them, "Suppose one of you has only one sheep and it falls into a pit on the sabbath; will you not lay hold of it and lift it out?" (Matthew 12:11)

Jesus immediately reached out his hand and caught him, saying to him, "You of little faith, why did you doubt?" (Matthew 14:31 – Peter's walking on the water to Jesus)

And becoming aware of it, Jesus said, "You of little faith, why are you talking about having no bread?" (Matthew 16:8)

"Do you still not perceive? Do you not remember the five loaves for the five thousand, and how many baskets you gathered?" (Matthew 16:9)

A Bond of Love

Dear God,
You have made us.
Red, yellow, brown, white and black,
tall and short, fat and thin,
rich and poor, young and old –
all are your children.
Teach us to cooperate rather than to compete,
to respect rather than to revile,
to forgive rather than condemn.
Your son turned from no one.
May we learn, like him, to be open
to the share of the divine
that you have implanted
in each of your sons and daughters.
And may we forge a bond of love
that will make a living reality
the Christian life in which we profess to believe.

Anonymous

business
education in the
jesuit tradition

Seven

In those days when there was again a great crowd without anything to eat, he called his disciples and said to them, "I have compassion for the crowd, because they have been with me now for three days and have nothing to eat. If I send them away hungry to their homes, they will faint on the way—and some of them have come from a great distance." His disciples replied, "How can one feed these people with bread here in the desert?" He asked them, "How many loaves do you have?" They said, "Seven." Then he ordered the crowd to sit down on the ground; and he took the seven loaves, and after giving thanks he broke them and gave them to his disciples to distribute; and they distributed them to the crowd. They had also a few small fish; and after blessing them, he ordered that these too should be distributed. They ate and were filled; and they took up the broken pieces left over, seven baskets full. Now there were about four thousand people. And he sent them away.

Mark 8:1-9

Business Education in the Jesuit Tradition

The following is excerpted from a talk given by Fr. Timothy Brown, S.J., to members of the faculty in the Sellinger School of Business, Loyola College, September 1988.

In a passage deleted from the selection, Fr. Brown cites from Robert Coles' The Moral Life of Children, *the story of Ruby Bridges. At six years of age, Ruby became the first black child admitted to her New Orleans school. Ruby's "moral stamina" – her smiles in the face of verbal abuse, and her prayers for those who made threats against her – make her, in her own mother's words, one of the people who "just put their lives on the line for what's right" even if they "may not be the ones who talk a lot or argue a lot for what's right."*

The following comments focus on the slippery relationship between "talking a lot" about values and preparing students to act virtuously in their professional careers. In tracing a relationship between "paying attention" to the life of moral complexity and becoming virtuous, Fr. Brown suggests that values education consists in developing "habits of virtue."

In teaching Law and Ethics, I aim not only to give students the skills they need for distinguished professional performance, but also to teach them to be leaders who are sensitive to justice and service and who can exercise their power with competence and compassion. As Father Arrupe wrote in 1973, "Today our prime educational objective must be to form men for others: men and women who cannot even conceive of love of God which does not include love for the least of their neighbors; men and women completely convinced that love of God which does not issue in Justice for the fellow human beings is a farce" (Men For Others," Justice, p. 124)

The main question I've been asking myself this past year, my first year teaching business ethics, has been: "How does a person become virtuous?" Aristotle said that one becomes virtuous by doing virtuous acts. One becomes brave by doing brave acts. One becomes kind by doing kind acts. So what exactly is the relationship between talking about good and bad and helping students to do good?

Some educators believe that ethics taught separately leads students to think of ethical behavior as something to be considered at one's leisure, not in real-world situations, i.e., that it leads to a kind of compartmentalization of values.

But I believe strongly that the explicit teaching of ethics can raise moral sensitivity. First of all, students want to know. I have had many MBA students approach me this past year to comment that the issues we had discussed in class had never been presented to them before anywhere. Some of the most challenging and perplexing of our discussions have concerned the role of the United States in Third World countries: How responsible are United States companies in Third World nations? Are working conditions safe? Are wages fair? Students also want to know about the ethics of the domestic marketplace: What about Wall Street issues regarding insider trading or the recent merger and acquisition mania? Perhaps most important of all, they want to know whether or not they are really being prepared for the tough ethical choices that they know they will have to make.

We should not, I think, ignore these students' need to address these questions. A number of Jesuits have been working for years in these areas, and in a recent General Congregation the attention of the entire Society of Jesus was brought to focus on the need to research and act in the following areas:

- the spiritual hunger of so many, particularly the young, who search for meaning and values in a technological culture;

- attacks by governments on human rights through assassination, imprisonment, torture, the denial of religious freedom and political expression;

- discrimination against whole categories of human beings such as migrants and racial or religious minorities;

– the unjust treatment and exploitation of women;

– public policies and social attitudes which threaten human life for the unborn, the handicapped and the aged; and

– economic oppression and spiritual needs of the unemployed, of poor and landless peasants, and of workers, with whom many Jesuits, like our worker priests, have identified themselves in order to bring them the good news (Companions of Jesus Sent into Today's World [Decree1] pars. 45 ff.).

Neither should we forget, however, merely addressing these issues is only half the battle. As Harvard President Derek Bok has commented, teaching students about ethical issues is likely to produce unethical behavior, if not outright cynicism, unless the institutions doing the teaching are themselves perceived as ethical, caring, and sensitive. Merely attempting to teach ethics in the classroom is inadequate. Institutions must also be prepared to set an example for their students. Jesuits who work in colleges can exercise a deep and lasting influence on their students and on a society as a whole by helping to raise faith and justice issues in their courses. From my classroom teaching experience, I have seen that students will admit that they are thinking about some particular issue for the first time or even admit that they haven't really decided on the question being asked. Students do have a sense of right and wrong with regard to being honest and respecting property rights. Applying these values to specific ethical choices is another matter. I believe that the attitudes they develop really become the critical factor in how they will behave in the future.

In the 19th century, ethics and values were required courses important enough to be taught by the college president. Furthermore, these courses were reinforced by a campus environment that viewed students' conduct and character as central to its mission. The schools founded by Ignatius of Loyola in the 16th century had a clear purpose: to form leaders who would carry forth into their personal and professional lives a mission of service to others. I think that this mission continues today, in our emphasis on such community values as equality of opportunity for all, the principles of distributive and social justice, and the attitude of mind that sees service to others, particularly the poor, as more self-fulfilling than success or prosperity. Jesuit education is preparation for active commitment. Without any attempt at manipulation, it tries to form men and women who will put their beliefs and attitudes into practice throughout their lives. That is why we have organized programs such as Project Baltimore as well, to get our students active in local services to the poor and deprived.

Education is not mere training. You go to school not for knowledge alone but to develop good habits: the habit of expression, the habit of attention, even the habit of being. In Art and Scholasticism, Jacques Maritain says, "Habits are interior growths of spontaneous life. . . [O]nly the living (that is to say, minds alone are perfectly alive) can acquire them, because they alone are capable of raising the level of their being by their own activity." Developing these habits of virtue is a full-time task, not to be restricted to a required course or two in ethics or values. It requires time and effort, practice and concentration, both inside and outside the classroom. Character is formed by practicing the habit of making good choices.

The habit I have found most essential in teaching ethics is the practice of paying attention. Simone Weil's autobiography, Waiting for God, contains an essay entitled "Reflections on the Right School Studies with a View of the Love of God." In this essay, Weil speaks of the development of the faculty of attention as the soul interest and real object of school studies pursued with a view to the love of God. Having myself studied for enough years, I was very much taken by her observations. Weil views attention as a kind of waiting and watching, a condition of suspended thought. The point of attending is to be open to receive truth. She is interested in developing an attitude, a habit of paying attention that I see as essential in making ethical decisions. The stress is on attention because prayer consists in just that – attention. Weil's point isn't that no matter what you are learning and for whatever purpose, the time and effort spent working is not wasted because the result will one day be discovered in prayer. But that is not all. She adds that "Not only does the love of God have attention for its substance; the love of our neighbor, which we know to be the same love, is made of this same substance. The capacity to give one's attention to a sufferer (to someone in need) is very rare and difficult – almost a miracle and nearly all those who think they have this capacity do not possess it. To give this kind of attention means being able to say to our neighbor: 'what are you going through?' And isn't that the essence of developing habits of good character? To be able to pay attention to another and ask 'What are you about?' " (Waiting for God, p.115).

In the long run, I tell my classes to pay attention to their consciences, to that still small voice that tells us "this is right and this is wrong." I would like for them to get into the habit of paying attention to that voice. St. Cyril of Jerusalem, instructing catechumens wrote: "The dragon sits by the side of the road watching those who pass. Beware lest he devour you. We go to the Father of Souls, but it is necessary to pass by the dragon." No matter what that dragon may take, it takes moral courage to pass by.

Timothy Brown, S.J.

Reflection

In the rush and busy-ness of your daily live, how do you stop to pay attention?

We are faced with choices – small and large – every day. What do you do to ensure you are making ethical choices?

Do you have an understanding of living wage? Do you promote living wage for all in your workplace?

Setting Hearts on Fire:
A Spirituality for Leaders

What makes a good leader? And what makes a good leader great? Jesus Christ was perhaps the greatest leader of all time. What made him a great leader? And what does reflecting upon Jesus' leadership model offer to today's leader? *Setting Hearts on Fire: A Spirituality for Leaders* looks at Jesus as leader – a leader who knew how to shape a vision, dialogue with people, provide hope, and offer the possibility for transformation.

The Great Leader: Is There A Formula?

Max DePree, Chairman and CEO of Herman Miller, gives a wise message. He believes that leadership is not a science or discipline, but rather an art that is felt, experienced, and created. He argues that humanistic and Christian values are at the heart of artful leadership.

But men and women find that it is not easy to articulate a leadership model when they are struggling to balance an authentic Christian life with a professional life in a world characterized by self-gratification, self-fulfillment and intolerance; where the poor, minorities and other powerless groups are virtually invisible; and where, all too often, the standard for success in business is profit, the bottom line, and, following a philosophy such as the one advocated by a popular bumper sticker, "He who has the most toys in the end – WINS!"

In this book we attempt to reflect on leadership models in light of the Christian spirit of leadership. We contend that the secular and spiritual dimensions converge and can be captured by anyone, taught to everyone, and denied to no one.

By reflecting on secular leadership models along with analysis and reflection on Christ's leadership style, leaders can grow in their interior peace and can be pillars of stability and calm in shaping and living the organizational life of the 1990s and into the next millennium.

It is essential that people renew their own hearts before attempting to transform anything external. After inward renewal, it is time for true leaders to turn outward and take action to become organizational and social change agents. But what is meant by transformational leadership vs. transactional leadership?

Transactional leadership is characterized by leaders making contacts to exchange economic, political, or psycho-social goods. It means listening, encouraging, and being tough if necessary. The transactional leader motivates followers by appealing to lower needs of self-interest. Supervisors pay or promote subordinates based on their efforts or other contributions to the organization. Politicians exchange contracts or positions for votes and campaign contributions. Ideally transactional leaders engage in exchanges that involve honesty, fairness, responsibility, and reciprocity.

In contrast, transformational leadership is a process by which "leaders and followers seek to raise one another to higher levels of morality and motivation" by leaders appealing to ideals and moral values such as freedom, justice, equality, peace, and humanitarianism. Transforming leaders and followers transcend daily responsibilities, unite purpose, and link power bases. This form of leadership leads to creating or renewing institutional purpose, shaping visions and values, and making the mission a living reality for all members of the organization. For the transforming leader no opportunity is too small, no forum too insignificant, no group too junior, no system or institution too tight to work with in achieving these high aspirations.

There are many transactional Christian leaders today: presidents, principals, provincials, shop stewards, supervisors, CEO's, and captains. Transactional leaders may be involved in social justice programs: setting up soup kitchens and shelters, counseling alcoholics and drug addicts, volunteering for hospice and senior citizens' programs, planning educational or liturgical programs, lobbying against unfair housing or for healthcare reform.

Transforming the leadership of a Christian leader, however, goes beyond being employed in social justice programs. It means recognizing the call of Christ to the ways of his Gospel. It is going aside, as Christ did, to spend time with God to listen to God's Spirit and learn from that (cf. Jn 14:26, 16:8). It is taking time to let the Spirit of God set one's own heart on fire before going out as a leader to transform and set the world on fire.

Something may prevent transactional leaders from recognizing the Risen Lord in themselves and others. The potential of these leaders for transforming leadership can be realized through prayer.

Blessings and transformation will continue for leaders as they continually praise God. By discerning and meeting the Spirit of truth in prayer, transforming leaders and followers reach new heights of leadership and empowerment, in attitudes, dialogue, emotional wisdom, renewal, in shaping visions, hope, integrity, and prayer.

Timothy Brown, S.J.
Patricia Sullivan, R.S.M.

Reflection

Are you an instrument of renewal for others? What can you do to renew yourself and others?

What situations do you create that exclude others? That empower others?

How do you integrate your spiritual life in your workday life?

How do you impart hope to others?

Are you a person of integrity?

Grant Me A Heart

Lord, grant me a holy heart
that sees always what is fine and pure
and is not frightened at the sight of sin
but creates order wherever it goes.
Grant me a heart that knows nothing
of boredom, weeping and sighing.
Let me not be too concerned
with the bothersome thing I call "myself."
Lord, give me a sense of humor
and I will find happiness of life
and profit for others.

St. Thomas More

_____stewardship_____

The Poor Widow's Contribution

He sat down opposite the treasury, and watched the crowd putting money into the treasury. Many rich people put in large sums. A poor widow came and put in two small copper coins, which are worth a penny. Then he called his disciples and said to them, "Truly I tell you, this poor widow has put in more than all those who are contributing to the treasury. For all of them have contributed out of their abundance; but she out of her poverty has put in everything she had, all she had to live on."

Mark 12:41-44

Stewardship

Stewardship: A Disciple's Response
U.S. Bishops' Letter
December 1992

Three convictions in particular underlie what we say in this pastoral letter.

1. Mature disciples make a conscious, firm decision, carried out in action, to be followers of Jesus Christ no matter the cost to themselves.

2. Beginning in conversion, change of mind and heart, this commitment is expressed not in a single action, nor even in a number of actions over a period of time, but in an entire way of life. It means committing one's very self to the Lord.

3. Stewardship is an expression of discipleship, with the power to change how we understand and live out our lives. Disciples who practice stewardship recognize God as the origin of life, the giver of freedom, the source of all they have and are and will be. They know themselves to be recipients and caretakers of God's many gifts. They are grateful for what they have received and eager to cultivate their gifts out of love for God and one another.

Although religious faith is a strong force in the lives of many Americans, our country's dominant secular culture often contradicts the values of the Judeo-Christian tradition. This is a culture in which destructive "isms" materialism, relativism, hedonism, individualism, consumerism exercise seductive, powerful influences. There is a strong tendency to privatize faith, to push it to the margins of society, confining it to people's hearts or, at best, their homes, while excluding it from the marketplace of ideas where social policy is formed and men and women acquire their view of life and its meaning.

Although religious people often speak about community, individualism infects the religious experience of many persons. Also, while many are generous in giving of themselves and their resources to the church, others do not respond to the needs in proportion to what they possess. The result now is a lack of resources which seriously hampers the church's ability to carry out its mission and obstructs people's growth as disciples.

This letter initiates a process of encouraging people to examine and interiorize stewardship's implications. At the start of this process it is important to lay out a comprehensive view of stewardship, a vision of a sharing, generous, accountable way of life rooted in Christian discipleship which people can take to heart and apply to the circumstances of their lives.

Jesus' invitation to follow him is addressed to people of every time and condition. As bishops, we wish to present a vision which suits the needs and problems of the church in our country today and speaks to those who practice Christian stewardship in their particular circumstances. As bishops, we recognize our obligation to be models of stewardship in all aspects of our lives.

The Call

The Christian vocation is essentially a call to be a disciple of Jesus. Christians are called to be good stewards of the personal vocations they receive. Each of us must discern, accept and live out joyfully and generously the commitments, responsibilities and roles to which God calls him or her. Every human life, every personal vocation, is unique. The vocations of all Christians do have elements in common. One of these is the call to be a disciple. Discipleship in this sense is Christian life. People do not hear the Lord's call in isolation from one another. Vocations are communicated, discerned, accepted and lived out within a community of faith which is a community of disciples; its members try to help one another hear the Lord's voice and respond.

Jesus not only calls people to him but also forms them and sends them out in his service. Being sent on a mission is a consequence of being a disciple. Becoming a disciple of Jesus Christ leads naturally to the practice of stewardship. These linked realities, discipleship and stewardship, then make up the fabric of a Christian life in which each day is lived in an intimate, personal relationship with the Lord.

Union with Christ gives rise to a sense of solidarity and common cause between the disciples and the Lord, and also among the disciples themselves. Christians must be stewards of their personal vocations, for it is these which show how, according to the circumstances of their individual lives, God wants them to cherish and service a broad range of interests and concerns: life and health, along with their own intellectual and spiritual well-being and that of others; material goods and resources; the natural environment; the cultural heritage of humankind.

"Without a vocation, man's existence would be meaningless. We have been created to bear the responsibility God has entrusted us with. Though different, each man should fulfill his specific vocation and shoulder his individual responsibility" (Anwar el-Sadat, In Search of Meaning, Harper and Row, 1977).

"Like duty, law, religion, the word vocation has a dull ring to it, but in terms of what it means, it is really not dull at all. Vocare, to call, of course, and man's vocation is a man's calling. It is the work that he is called to in this world, the thing that he is summoned to spend his life doing. We can speak of a man's choosing his vocation, but perhaps it is at least as accurate to speak of a vocation's choosing the man, of a call's being given and a man's hearing it, or not hearing it. And maybe that is the place to start: the business of listening and hearing. A man's life is full of all sorts of voices calling him in all sorts of directions. Some of them are voices from inside and some of them are voices from outside. The more alive and alert we are, the more clamorous our lives are. Which do we listen to? What kind of voice do we listen for?" (Frederick Buechner, The Hungering Dark, Seabury Press, 1981).

Jesus' Way

Jesus is the supreme teacher of Christian stewardship, as He is of every other aspect of Christian life; and in Jesus' teaching and life, self-emptying is fundamental. His self-emptying is not sterile self-denial for its own sake; rather, in setting aside self, he is filled with the Father's will. In calling disciples, Jesus empowers them to collaborate with him in the work of redemption for themselves and on behalf of others. The Beatitudes and the rest of the Sermon on the Mount prescribe the lifestyle of a Christian disciple (cf. Mt. 5:3-7:27).

An oikonomos or steward is one to whom the owner of a household turns over responsibility for caring for the property, managing affairs, making resources yield as much as possible and sharing the resources with others. The position involves trust and accountability.

A parable near the end of Matthew's Gospel (cf. Mt. 25:14-30) gives insight into Jesus' thinking about stewards and stewardship. It is the story of a man who was going on a journey and who left his wealth in silver pieces to be tended by three servants. Two of them respond wisely, the third foolishly. The silver pieces of this story stand for a great deal besides money. All temporal and spiritual goods are created by and come from God. That is true of everything human beings have: spiritual gifts like faith, hope and love, talents of body and brain, cherished relationships with family and friends, material goods, the achievements of human genius and skill, the world itself. One day God will require an accounting of the use each person has made of the particular portion of these goods entrusted to him or her. Each will be measured by the standard of his or her individual vocation. He will judge individuals according to what they have done with what they were given. St. Ignatius understood that the right use of things includes and requires that they be used to serve others.

To be a Christian disciple is a rewarding way of life, a way of companionship with Jesus, and the practice of stewardship as a part of it is itself a source of deep joy. Human activity is valuable both for what it accomplishes here and now and also for its relationship to the hereafter. It stresses not only the discontinuity between here and now and hereafter, but also the astonishing fact of continuity.

God's kingdom already is present in history, imperfect but real. To be sure, it will come to fulfillment by God's power, on his terms, in his own good time. And yet, by their worthy deeds in this life, people also make a limited but real human contribution to building up the kingdom. The purpose of the human vocation to earthly service of one's fellow human beings is precisely to make ready the material of the celestial realm (Gaudium et Spes). In Christ, God has entered fully into human life and history. For one who is Christ's disciple there is no dichotomy, and surely no contradiction, between building the kingdom and serving human purposes as a steward does. The "life to come" is in continuity with this present life through the human goods, the worthy human purposes, which people foster now. And after people have done their best, God will perfect human goods and bring about the final fulfillment of human persons.

Living as a Steward

God wishes human beings to be his collaborators in the work of creation, redemption and sanctification; and such collaboration involves stewardship in its most profound sense. People are called to cooperate with the Creator in continuing the divine work. Stewardship of creation is one expression of this. God's mandate to humankind to collaborate with him in the task of creating the command to work comes before the fall. Work is a fundamental aspect for human happiness and fulfillment. It is intrinsic to responsible stewardship of the world.

Christians see human achievements as "a sign of God's greatness and the flowering of his own mysterious design" (Gaudium et Spes, 34). Human cooperation with God's work of creation in general takes several forms. One of these is a profound reverence for the great gift of life, their own lives and the lives of others, along with readiness to spend themselves in serving all that preserves and enhances life. This reverence and readiness begin with opening one's eyes to how precious a gift life really is and that is not easy, in view of our tendency to take the gift for granted.

Partly, too, stewardship of the world is expressed by jubilant appreciation of nature, whose God-given beauty not even exploitation and abuse have destroyed. Ecological stewardship means cultivating a heightened sense of human interdependence and solidarity. It therefore calls for renewed efforts to address what Pope John Paul II called "the structural forms of poverty" existing in this country and on the international level. Especially this form of stewardship requires that many people adopt simpler lifestyles. As Pope John Paul says, "Simplicity, moderation and discipline, as well as a spirit of sacrifice, must become a part of everyday life, lest all suffer the negative consequences of the careless habits of a few" (Message for the World Day of Peace, Jan. 1, 1990).

Life as a Christian steward also requires continued involvement in the human vocation to cultivate material creation. So-called ordinary work offers as many opportunities as do supposedly more glamorous occupations. A woman who works at a supermarket checkout counter writes: "I feel that my job consists of a lot more than ringing up orders, taking people's money and bagging their groceries...By doing my job well, I know I have a chance to do God's work too. Because of this, I try to make each of my customers feel special. While I'm serving them, they become the most important people in my life" (Maxine F. Dennis, in Of Human Hands).

Everyone has some natural responsibility for a portion of the world and an obligation in caring for it to acknowledge God's dominion. But there are also those who might be called stewards by grace. Baptism makes Christians stewards of this kind. We find the perfect model of such stewardship in the Lord. Although Jesus is the unique priest and mediator, His disciples share in his priestly work. Participation in Christ's redemptive activity extends even, though certainly not only, to the use people make of experiences which otherwise might seem the least promising: deprivation, loss, pain.

Penance also belongs to this aspect of Christian life. Through penance voluntarily accepted one gradually becomes liberated from those obstacles to Christian discipleship which a secularized culture exalting individual gratification places in one's way. Sin causes people to turn in on themselves; to become grasping and exploitative toward possessions and other people; to grow accustomed to conducting relationships not by the standards of generous stewardship but by the calculus of self-interest: "What's in it for me?" Constantly Christians must beg God for the grace of conversion: the grace to know who they are, to whom they belong, how they are to live the grace to repent and change and grow, the grace to become good disciples and stewards.

Thus, the stewardship of disciples is not reducible only to one task or another. It involves embracing, cultivating, enjoying, sharing and sometimes also giving up the goods of human life. The human goods Christians cherish and cultivate will be perfected and they themselves will be fulfilled in that kingdom, already present, which Christ will bring to perfection and one day hand over to the Father.

Stewards of the Church

"When I began to provide dental treatment for persons with AIDS, I knew HIV-positive people desperately needed this ser-

vice, but I did not know how much I needed them. Time and again, reaching out to serve and heal, I have found myself served and healed. Their courage, compassion, wisdom and faith have changed my life. I have faced my own mortality, and I rejoice in the daily gift of life. My love for people has taken on new dimensions. I hug and kiss my wife and family more than ever and see them as beautiful gifts from God. My ministry as a deacon has become dynamic, and I regard my profession as a vital part of it."
- Dr. Anthony M. Giambalvo, Rockville Centre, N.Y.

The new covenant in and through Christ, the reconciliation he effects between humankind and God forms a community: the new people of God, the body of Christ, the church. The unity of this people is itself a precious good, to be cherished, preserved and built up by lives of love. But how is the church built up? Through personal participation in and support of the church's mission of proclaiming and teaching, serving and sanctifying. It is within the power of disciples, and a duty, that they be generous stewards of the church, giving freely of their time, talent and treasure.

In various ways, then, stewardship of the church leads people to share in the work of evangelization or proclaiming the good news, and in works of justice and mercy on behalf of persons in need. The most basic and pervasive obstacle to human solidarity is sheer selfish lack of love, a lack which people must acknowledge and seek to correct when they find it in their own hearts and lives. Extreme disparities in wealth and power block unity and communion. Such disparities exist today between person and person, social class and social class, nation and nation.

Social justice, which the pastoral letter "Economic Justice for All" calls a kind of contributive justice, is a particular aspect of the virtue of solidarity. It gives moral as well as economic content to the concept of productivity. Thus productivity "cannot be measured solely by its output of goods and services." Rather, "patterns of productivity must ... be measured in light of their impact on the fulfillment of basic needs, employment levels, patterns of discrimination, environmental impact and sense of community" ("Economic Justice for All," 72).

Finally, and most poignantly, solidarity is obstructed by the persistence of religious conflicts and divisions. Our individual lives as disciples and stewards must be seen in relation to God's larger purposes: to make many one. Those who heed this call find their hearts and minds expanding to embrace all men and women, especially those in need, in a communion of mercy and love.

The eucharist is the great sign and agent of this expansive communion of charity. Here Christ's love indeed, his very self flows into his disciples and, through them and their practice of stewardship, to the entire human race. Through the eucharistic celebration, disciples give thanks to God for gifts received and strive to share them with others. The eucharist is the sign and agent of that heavenly communion in which we shall together share, enjoying the fruits of stewardship. It is not only the promise but the commencement of the heavenly banquet where human lives are perfectly fulfilled.

The Christian Steward

"I was suddenly confronted with serious surgery, which I never thought would happen to me. It always happened to others. I recall vividly the days before the surgery. I really received the grace to ask myself, 'What do I own, and what owns me?'

"When you are wheeled into a surgery room, it really doesn't matter who you are or what you possess. What counts is the confidence in a competent surgical staff and a good and gracious God.

"I know that my whole understanding and appreciation of the gifts and resources I possess took on new meaning. It is amazing how a divine economy of life and health provide a unique perspective of what really matters." - Archbishop Thomas Murphy of Seattle

Good stewards understand that they are to share with others what they have received, that this must be done in a timely way and that God will hold them accountable for how well or badly they do it. In the lives of disciples, something else must come before the practice of stewardship. They need a flash of insight, a certain way of seeing by which they view the world and their relationship to it in a fresh, new light. More than anything else, it may be this glimpse of the divine grandeur in all that is which sets people on the path of Christian stewardship.

Not only in material creation do people discern God present and active, but also, and especially, in the human heart. Christian stewards are conscientious and faithful. They are generous out of love as well as duty. The life of a Christian steward, lived in imitation of the life of Christ, is challenging, even difficult in many ways; but both here and hereafter it is charged with intense joy.

After Jesus, it is the Blessed Virgin Mary who by her example most perfectly teaches the meaning of discipleship and stewardship in their fullest sense. All of their essential elements are found in her life: She was called and gifted by God, she responded generously, creatively and prudently, she understood her divinely assigned role as "handmaid" in terms of service and fidelity. In light of this, it only remains for all of us to ask ourselves this question: Do we also wish to be disciples of Jesus Christ? The Spirit is ready to show us the way, a way of which stewardship is a part.

It is a central part of the human vocation that we be good stewards of what we have received – this garden, this divine-human workshop, this world and all that is in it – setting minds and hearts and hands to the task of creating and redeeming in cooperation with our God, creator and Lord of all.

Reflection

How do you live out your discipleship in your daily interactions with others?

How are you open to fulfilling your vocation as disciple, to shouldering your individual responsibility?

In your work, can you claim the same dedication of service to others as the supermarket worker mentioned above?

How do you break through your self-imposed barriers to become a man or woman for others?

The Faithful Stewards

The faithful all lived together and owned everything in common: they sold their goods and possessions and shared out the proceeds amongst themselves according to what each needed. They went as a body to the temple every day but met in their houses for the breaking of the bread. They shared their goods gladly and generously. They praised God and were looked up to by everyone. Day by day the Lord added to their community those destined to be saved.

Acts 2:44-47

Ethical Issues and Stewardship

Adam and Eve became the first stewards when they were instructed to look after the fish and the birds, and "every living thing that moves on the earth." The Greek word for steward is "epitropos" – it means one to whose care or honor anything has been entrusted, a curator, or guardian, a manager of a household or of lands, one who has the care and tutelage of children. Two Hebrew words relate to stewardship. The first – "mesheq" comes from an unused root meaning "to hold." The second "cakan" means of use or service or profit or benefit. Webster tells us that steward comes from old English "Stig" meaning hall and "weard" meaning keeper. A steward in modern usage is a person put in charge of a large estate or an administrator of finances and property.

Stewards have an obligation to take care of all the resources given to them. What constitutes good stewardship? Good stewardship is the key to giving fuller expression to what is at the heart of our solidarity in the evangelization that we are one body in Christ. The role of stewardship is precisely because man and women are created in God's image and likeness.

In Genesis 1:26-28, they are to "exercise dominion over creation and to live in solidarity." Jesus himself in Luke 19:1-28 calls his disciples, rich and poor, to good stewardship. In Peter 4:10, we read "as each one has received a gift, use it to serve one another as good stewards of God's varied graces." In the Book of Leviticus, you will find the Lord speaking to Moses on Mount Sinai and instructing him to tell the Israelites that "the land belongs to me, and to me you are only strangers and guests"(Lev 25:23).

The idea of stewardship incorporates this guest relationship, which characterizes those of us on the land who are entrusted with the wealth that belongs to God. We own nothing absolutely; we are stewards. As St. Paul remarks in I Corinthians 4:2, "what is expected of stewards is that each one should be found worthy of his or her trust."

In "At Home in the Web of Life," the Catholic Bishops of Appalachia wrote the following on Catholic Social Teaching as it applies to stewardship.

Human Dignity

The first principle is human dignity. This principle reflects the biblical teaching that we humans are made in the image of God. Human dignity is a key ethical foundation for sustainable community. Because of God's image within us, every human person has the right to all that is needed to guarantee human dignity.

Community

The second principle is community, sometimes referred to as "the common good," expressed at every level from the family to the whole human race, including Earth's whole community of life. The principle of community flows from the revelation that God is a community, a Trinity of three persons in one: Father, Son and Holy Spirit.

Our human dignity can never be separated from community with our sisters and brothers, or from our community with the rest of creation. We are never solely individuals, devoted only to competition and selfishness. Rather we are always members of community, truly responsible for our sisters and brothers, and also for God's sacred Earth.

Ecology

Human dignity and community are linked with the wider dignity and community of nature in the single web of life. We may describe this reality as a sixth principle, the natural order of creation.

To follow the natural order of creation, economics should not undermine human dignity and community, nor the dignity and community of nature. It needs to remains rooted in the web of life, according to natural and social ecology.

If we fail to care for our precious earth and for the poor, then creation itself will rebel against us. Further, to undermine nature and the poor is to reject the word of God in creation. Deep within the ecological crisis lies the spiritual error called materialism. Materialism does not reverence God's creation. Instead it abuses creation. Cut off from God's presence in creation, the materialistic spirit grows destructive.

In the Jesuit documents on justice, effective social transformation in promotion of social justice and the good community requires systematic action on the level of economic and political structures. But more is needed, because those economic and political structures are themselves rooted in social and cultural values and attitudes. Accordingly, full human liberation for all people demands the development of communities of solidarity at the grass roots level where we can all work together – as partners – towards total human development. In the spirit of Jesus' recognition of his disciples as friends rather than servants (John 15:15), the call to solidarity demands that we enter into a relationship and live as the friends, not simply the helpers, of those with whom we serve. This solidarity exists when there are sustainable, mutual, respectful relationships between diverse people who all experience themselves as brothers and sisters, all children of the living God in our midst.

Stewardship

The proper purpose of education is to give greater honor and glory to God by ennobling humanity.

In the words of St. Ignatius:
Do not speak
Do not reply
Do not meditate
Do not go abroad
Indeed do nothing without first asking yourself:
Does this please God; is this an example that will edify
    my neighbors?

Reflection

What does it mean to you to be a good steward?

Are you a good steward of human dignity? Of community? Of creation?

Can you visualize what a world of good stewardship would look like?

What may be the major obstacle in your life to practicing stewardship?

Eyes of Our Heart

May the Lord Jesus touch our eyes,
as He did those of the blind.
Then we shall begin to see
in visible things those which are invisible.
May He open our eyes to gaze,
not on present realities,
but on the blessings to come.
May He open the eyes of our heart
to contemplate God in Spirit,
through Jesus Christ the Lord, to whom belong
power and glory through all eternity.

Origen

conclusion

While I Was Still Young

While I was still young, before I went on my travels,
I sought wisdom openly in my prayer.
Before the temple I asked for her,
and I will search for her until the end.

From the first blossom to the ripening grape
my heart delighted in her;
my foot walked on the straight path;
from my youth I followed her steps.

I inclined my ear a little and received her,
and I found for myself much instruction.
I made progress in her;
to him who gives wisdom I will give glory.

For I resolved to live according to wisdom,
and I was zealous for the good,
and I shall never be disappointed.
My soul grappled with wisdom,
and in my conduct I was strict;

I spread out my hands to the heavens,
and lamented my ignorance of her.
I directed my soul to her,
and in purity I found her.

With her I gained understanding from the first;
therefore I will never be forsaken.
My heart was stirred to seek her;
therefore I have gained a prize possession.
The Lord gave me my tongue as a reward,
and I will praise him with it.

Draw near to me, you who are uneducated,
and lodge in the house of instruction.
Why do you say you are lacking in these things,

and why do you endure such great thirst?
I opened my mouth and said,
Acquire wisdom for yourselves without money.

Put your neck under her yoke,
and let your souls receive instruction;
it is to be found close by.

Sirach 51: 13-26

The Face of Jesus

Loving God, we have all we need and want: food, drink, and clothing; welcoming care and visitation. Within this unity of needs and desires, help us to be more gentle with each other, and more open to our unity with our sisters and brothers all over this planet, whose faces we see as the face of Jesus. Amen.

Printed in the United States
72588LV00002B/1-99